Drop your noise

59 ways to find the hidden power to speak in our sensitivities

2

KD has the moral right to be identified as the author of this book in accordance with the Copyright, Designs and Patents Act 1988.

No part of this book may be reproduced, distributed, or transmitted in any form or by any means, including photocopying, recording, or other electronic or mechanical methods, without the prior written permission of the publisher, except in the case of brief quotations embodied in critical reviews and certain other non-commercial uses permitted by copyright law.

.

Copyright © 2024, Kirtana168 ltd

Published by: Kirtana168

Cover design by: Kirtana168

First Edition

Printed in United Kingdom

Editing by Jill Segal

For more information, please visit: www.Kirtana168.com

There is empathy.

There is equity.

Then there is the power of equanimity.

To Mom- Thank you. Love you. In eternal appreciation.

Drop your noise

59 ways to find
the hidden power
to speak in our sensitivities

Introduction

Hi, I'm Kirti the author of this book and **#Befriendurmind,** originally published back in 2016. As a communication strategist, I speak and facilitate conversations around complex matters of the heart and mind.

My intention wasn't to write an elaborate wordy book. But to share simple wisdom that has supported me on my project to discover my style of calm communication.

It all started with the power of enquiry, trusting by questioning myself again and again. I noticed that our inner truth gets buried under layers upon layers of knowledge with easy access of social media, where we struggle to separate what's true from fake. This constant consumption of knowledge disconnects us from our own inner truth so we end up speaking in cliches even though our actions tell us a different story. In today's modern world, while we have become so aware of each other's differences which should feel like a sense of belonging, we find ourselves more divided and concerned how to connect to each other. Communication through our differences feels really tough.

Based on my experience working with clients from different multi-ethnic communities on their stress and ability to express themselves with ease, in this condensed book I want to share with you something called slogans. They are short reminders to train our mind to speak calmly to each other, especially in our differences. It's based on the idea of equanimity, which means staying calm and balanced, even when things are tough.

These slogans are a tool to train our mind to be more observant and inquire into the quality of our thoughts, emotions and communication. By doing so, it gives us the confidence to find our own truth. Free us from self-judgements which may have been holding us back from enjoying our quality of life.

While some of these sections may feel repetitive, the aim is to support you and strengthen your nerves until that calm communication has settled within yourself.

I take absolutely no offense if you leave it in the bathroom for distraction-free reading!

Fair warning - this book may feel like it's ripping off the band-aid, challenging what you've convinced yourself is your truth. But if you allow yourself to start the power of internal examination, a shift is possible.

Sales pitch here: if you would like me to deliver a workshop, talk or speak at your event, contact me on befriendyourmind@kirtana168.com

Or scan the QR code for more.

How can we be more thoughtful about our way of communication?

Sometimes when we look inside our own habitual thoughts, when we are feeling uncertain how to approach life's challenges, the worst part of us shows up. We can be defensive, avoid or procrastinate making a decision. Often, we are caught between what we should do and what we really want to do. If we choose the 'should' road, very often it may lead us on a path of mishaps, misunderstandings and misjudgements.

Why do we do this?

The truth is we yearn to feel a sense of belonging, it's what makes us human. Belonging is often seen as having shared values and beliefs. However, the problem happens when we don't share the same way of expressing it. When this happens, without realising it, we hold back from being ourselves, by repressing our true thoughts in favour of 'thinking to do the right thing'. We don't know how to find the middle ground between the 'should do' and who we truly want to be, in a situation.

By taking this approach, we may feel constantly edgy and often confused, as we face the discomforts of our own internal dialogue about our principles, traditions and values, conflicting with those of others. This discomfort taints our sense of seeing situations clearly and objectively.

Let's say an unexpected situation shows up in our outer circumstances, for example: sudden loss of financial income, death or being made redundant. How we are conditioned through our life experiences and upbringing, influences the way we react towards it. We greet it with different flavours of reaction: aversion or affection, reflecting discomfort, resistance, or indulgence.

We don't realise it that we have been doing this for long, so it's habitual not characteristic. If unchecked, in the long run, we alone continue to be contributors to undesirable outcomes: socially, economically or politically.

What can be done to change this?

Breaking free from this mindset, is life-changing and it takes practice, not just knowledge.

First, by recognising our self-aversion or self-affections, we no longer skip being aware of others but also manage our personal agenda more attentively and thoughtfully. We give ourselves the chance to see our invisible fears or attachment to the outcome we want.

Secondly, we become aware of ourselves, by stepping back from our thoughts and becoming an observer of ourselves. This is an opportunity to see what's underneath our 'conditioning', or what I call the 'make-up' of our identity. This is where we can see the naked truth of who we are, as we are and how we engage with the mixture of culture, social and intellectual conditioning. By seeing this, we become 'okay' to recognise that others experience it in their way, too.

The importance of this, especially in today's world, is to strive towards being thoughtful on navigating the complexities of our own identities, especially around the identities of others, with a sense of respect and dignity.

Thirdly, which is vital to communicating in different communities, we have to bear in mind the importance of dignity. It's the secret to true belonging. The way to achieve this is with a calm sense of discernment.

This will reflect relevancy, relatability and consideration. With this kind of practice, we build our resilience by having the ability to sit with what we disagree, what we want to run from and consider other perspectives. This requires a constant practice of looking within, so that we form our lens of being, we understand our doing, and start to consider how we talk to one another.

If you want to take anything away from this book, this is it: **Rip the band aid off.**

1. Recognise our aversions, affections and apprehensions. Instead of asking "Why me?" consider "Why not me?"

2. Don't run from self-judgment and the discomfort of differences. Remove the facade of empathy, the disguises of self-pity and the attachment to our righteousness.

3. Accept, then apply a sense of objectivity and discernment. Don't dwell on what does not serve purpose, see the little details that make the positive change.

I always remind myself: beneath our identity- be what we always are and let doing come and go.

59

Why 59?

I'm always asked why 59? I wrote this book based upon my previous work "#befriendurmind", 59 ways to observe your mind without meditation. In the first book, I provided practical slogans for observing our habitual thought patterns to cut through old expectations, assumptions and aversions that prevent us from feeling contentment.

Inspired by Buddhist mind training for loving kindness, I train my mind, on certain areas of my life with 59 slogans. Slogans are short phrases that provide practical ways to consistently train one's introspection with the aim of communicating with more compassion and ease - with ourselves and others.

Also, a number like 59 is a transitional number. My podcast guest, Tom Verghese, spoke of this in our talk on 'conscious aging'. "Think about the year before major milestones in life - the years before we turn 30, 40, 50 and 60, many of us undergo a search for our meaning. These are times we naturally reflect back and also look ahead to how we want to live".

To maximise these slogans:

Take one a week, and apply it to your life. Reflect on it, notice when the opportunities arise where you can apply it. Unlike mindfulness, where you label the thoughts as 'thinking', in this practice, notice the quality of it and observe how it influences you from within and your surroundings.

17

Reminders

1. Stay true, stay aligned, stay authentic

When we discuss alignment, we are emphasising the importance of staying true to our purpose, acting with integrity and embodying authenticity. It's crucial to recognise that these elements don't always align perfectly. They are in constant fluctuation depending on the situation or relationship. When they are out of sync, we often encounter issues like miscommunication, misunderstandings or misjudgements.

To truly align ourselves, we must reflect on our thoughts, emotions and communication with honesty.

Self-examining these three allows us to uncover or notice any manipulative tendencies or hidden intentions beneath seemingly good deeds.

1. Is it true?
2. Is it aligned with my integrity?
3. Am I being motivated by a desire for validation or recognition?

Even if our actions appear positive on the surface, any deceitful or ulterior motives can ultimately harm others.

Strive for transparency to reveal your truth.

2. Examine-Focus-Understand

Communication, at its core, is a combination of thoughts, emotions, and words. These elements are shaped by our past experiences, perceptions and conditioning.

Through that within us, we shape our principles, values and beliefs, which serves us well or are harmful, depending on how we choose to engage with our interactions.

Often if we don't attend to our communication, we can find ourselves in an inner conflict about how to express ourselves. This is often the case when we find ourselves in a mixture of different religions, generations, cultures, genders and all their possible complexities. We feel at odds on how to find common ground to fulfil a common purpose, be it a goal or an aspiration, we may be at odds with one another.

To understand the complexities of one another:

1. Examine and understand our personal interpretations, their significance and how it affects one another.
2. Focus on the patience to attend to quality of our thoughts. By reframing our thoughts and our choice of thoughts, we are more skilful with our dialogue as it has a profound effect on others' interpretation and contribution to decisions and choices.
3. Understand your emotions. Thoughts alone don't have an effect; it's combined with the energy of emotions. Emotions are the energy force behind the way we express those thoughts and lets the recipients sense their safety and manage their well-being.

So always focus on 3 areas: how we talk to ourselves, how we speak about ourselves and how we interact with others.

3. Acknowledge, gentleness and letting go

When you decide to change your communication style, it's important to:

1. Acknowledge any limitations you may have in how you currently communicate.

Instead of trying to control or hide the limitations, be precise in identifying them and accepting them as they are.

2. Practice gentleness with yourself in your self-talk and interactions. Often gentleness is seen as a sign of weakness, why not view it as a quiet strength?

Instead of using harsh or critical language towards yourself, approach your thoughts and feelings with objective kindness and understanding. By being harsh with ourselves, it's likely we treat other circumstances, unknowingly, with the same attitude. In the long run this rarely succeeds.

3. Learn to let go of the need to control every aspect of a situation or conversation. Trying to force a specific outcome will only lead to frustration and lack of clarity. Being true with uncertainty brings accuracy.

Instead, practice strengthening the skill of patience, humility, and the ability to observe and understand before taking action. This will allow understanding a situation to take place, consider all aspects and know when to act and when to step back.

4. Be ok to be un-okay

Life is far from perfect - but then again, what is perfect, really?

We all experience discomfort and struggle in our lives, and there's no manual on how to navigate it all. It's important to remember that discomfort is just a fleeting moment, a nudge to stop and reflect on how we can respond differently to life's challenges.

Ultimately, how we choose to behave in the face of chaos, challenges and complexity is up to us. So, be okay with not being okay - embrace the discomfort and find your own path through it.

5. Don't kid yourself

Stop trying to deceive others to avoid feeling like a bad person. Embrace your true thoughts and feelings without judgment.

1. It's okay to acknowledge them without feeling the need to share, justify or fake them.
2. Lean into the honesty of the desire to try to cover it up.
3. Notice the physical discomfort and stay focused with a 3 minute breathe before going into reframing your state of mind.

Steps to breathe into discomfort:

1. Place a timer for 3- 5 minutes.
2. Preferably, sit or lie down.
3. Lean back and place your hands behind your head.
4. Breathe in, and feel your ribcage expand.
5. Exhale, long, imagine your fatigue leaving your body.
6. Don't rush between your inhalations and exhalations.

6. Lighten-up those damn fears

When sitting quietly with inner thoughts, embrace the rising discomfort ones with light-hearted humour. We are much harder on ourselves than on others. So don't be surprised, when you try the humour approach that:

1. It may be uncomfortable at first, the mind tries to act tough about everything and tell you to suck it up to be strong.
2. You may experience intense self-criticism or fear the sensation of failure or rejection.
3. You may feel waves of guilt and shame at times, as the mind justifies these feelings, like a parent telling you a good ol' "I told you so".

Remind yourself to approach these moments with a touch of humour. Light hearted-ness, is that 'aaah I see you, and wow you sound intense' approach. Greet it with light-heartedness, not in a self -deprecating way to hide or mask the feeling.

Lighten the heaviness to inspire the strength to navigate through your darkest habits and secrets. Instead of focusing on finding a solution, be curious about your thoughts and feelings, as they are temporary. Breathe life into your journey called life, don't wait till the end to wish you did it differently. This attitude will help you see challenges as opportunities for growth, rather than dead ends or stress.

7. Find curiosity in the judgment

Our thoughts are fluid and constantly evolving, shaping how we see others. When we fixate on a single thought, it can become rigid like a stone, leading to hasty judgments and closing our minds to new perspectives.

Consider someone we dislike or see as "toxic". Labelling them as "bad" prompts us to seek evidence confirming our bias. This can result in gossip and reinforcement of our existing beliefs, creating a bubble of like-minded individuals.

But have you ever considered the impact of perpetuating that single thought may have on someone else's well-being?

Think about this: our relationships reflect how tightly we hold onto thoughts, the energy we invest in them and their effect on others. Since thoughts aren't permanent, we have the opportunity to examine and adjust them for our own well-being and that of others.

Challenge your judgments with curiosity.

8. Balance the mental bank account

Think of your thoughts like a bank account - "cha Chang or oh shit, "... thoughts are informative. We love, love numbers in this modern world, so when you look at your quality of thoughts, they are like your assets, investments or liabilities.

Asset thoughts:

The ones that motivate and guide you productively. When you let these thoughts shift and evolve naturally over time, they remain useful and positive. Pay attention that they appreciate and don't depreciate.

Investment thoughts:

The thoughts time is spent on will have a return of investment on the action. They will be beneficial, giving direction and purpose, but if you invest in a thought that has a negative impact on others, be sure that it will come with an undesirable outcome, too.

Liability thoughts:

When thoughts become too fixed and controlling, they turn into liabilities and don't serve you. A classic example is perfectionist mindset - trying to manage life's natural chaos and change through rigid determination, no longer pays dividends.

The key is to hold your thoughts lightly and thoughtfully. Allow them to deepen and transform as life unfolds. Adaptability and self-examination keep your mental bank account in balance and let your thoughts work for you, not against you.

9. In chaos find calmness

Give yourself permission to view emotions as valuable feedback rather than constantly analysing or judging them. Emotions have the power to either weigh us down or lift us up, as they are intricately connected to our energetic system which serves as a bridge between our thoughts and physical body. They serve as messages to guide us.

Measure the quality of emotions as though it's on a spectrum, ranging from heavy and dull to fast-paced and anxious.

In moments of confusion, doubt, anger, or other challenging mental states, it is essential to:

1. Assess where you fall on the emotional spectrum
2. Notice the quality of emotions, to relax intentionally for change to happen
3. Pay attention to them as guideposts as you relax from their intensity to reach a state of neutrality
4. Only when resting in neutrality, is there clarity for decision-making and self-reflection.

Strive to reach the ideal place for our emotional health. Generally, it's found in the middle of this spectrum.

10. Slow down - sip in

Slow down and sip in. When faced with discomfort, resist the urge to react hastily. Take a moment to carefully examine the situation instead of immediately victimising yourself. Discomfort forces us to confront feelings we may try to avoid or suppress.

Remember to walk away, sit down, or simply take a deep breath.

The breath acts as an agent between our thoughts and actions, helping to calm our emotions when they threaten to overwhelm us.

Ideal is to breathe for up to 3 minutes.

Using your breath, inhaling 3 times and then empty the lungs with one long exhalation.

This is how you do it:

1. Clear your lungs out with a long exhale.
2. Sip in your first inhale down into the belly.
3. Sip in the second inhale into your lower lungs.
4. Sip in the third inhale to fill the top of chest.
5. When you do this, make sure the body expands and not contracts.
6. Then take a long breath out from chest, lower lungs then belly. Imagine emptying out air.
7. Repeat.

11. Welcome the unwelcome

Communication becomes stressful when the narrative of a situation is out of control. Think of it this way, have you ever attended an event only to have an uninvited guest make it very uncomfortable and worst of all you can't throw them out. We think the best way to handle this is to be rational, yet silently we are dealing with our state of panic or despair towards uncertainty, change or the unexpected. We feel out of control with this situation.

This is the same and the uncomfortable truth when we haven't deliberately practiced synchronising our mind with emotions. We struggle to be truly rational, or fail to reason calmly, because it's our resistance of the aversion (who is the unwelcome guest) that's driving us.

How do you welcome the unwelcome?

In every situation of aversion, recognising our aversion is where the growth resides. If we recognise it for what it is, we can navigate ourselves easier when other unexpected moments arrive in life. After all, how we respond to our situations makes all the difference.

Try this:

1. Identify the quality of aversion: its structure, and where you are physically holding it.
2. Aversion has an emotional weight from intense aggressive to passive aggressive. It's also on a spectrum, the full range - from desperation to depression and all in between. Notice the weight.
3. Slow down the aggression of aversion. Neutralise with slow physical movements and deliberate breaths. Exercises like tai-chi, and slow yoga can

make a difference.

By practicing this consistently, over time, we gain access to emotional regulation to greet those unwelcoming guests with welcoming arms.

12. Move from 'sit and stew'

Have you ever met individuals who are always talking about the problem and rarely about a solution?

Such individuals have a tendency to stew on the struggles, and staying with a repetitive sabotaging cycle. They consistently use phrases like: "The problem is..." even when a solution has been proposed.

By sitting consistently on the same thought with a sense of hopelessness and despair, they get stuck in their own way, agonising over consequences that may never happen and intensify self-judgment when facing adversity. Not only do they delay decisions, they also deplete their emotional energy and procrastinate, until a situation escalates.

How do you move away from this 'sit and stew' mindset?

Try this:

1. Recognise the quality of language used. Does it reflect limitations and reasons why a solution is not possible? The obstacle is not the problems themselves, but it's the tunnel vision of using words that only reflect impossibilities.
2. Avoid trying to quiet the mind through meditation. It may feel like an amplification of the noise of self-judgement. It can accelerate such a mind to fixate even more on a problem.
3. Lighten the heavy energy of resignation and depression. Engage in mindfulness while in motion - go for a walk, dance, or take photographs. Take up a creative activity that occupies your senses to see the beauty of moments and shifts your focus outward.

4. Avoid forcing gratitude. By moving, we can train our sense to see appreciation. Meet hopelessness and despair with a 'seeing is believing' approach.

By taking these small steps towards positivity and consistency in acknowledging the good in life, we can begin to shift our mindset towards finding solutions.

13. In control when out of control

Anxiety can feel like a whirlwind pulling you into the uncertain future. Anxiety has a quality of high speed, a feeling one has to react in a rush to establish some quick certainty. Certainty has two driving elements: expectation and assumption. Without our ability to be ok with them being challenged, we can find ourselves uncontrollably spiralling down with an intense physical urgency to control the shape of the outcome.

So how do we find centeredness to stay calm in the midst of the chaos?

1. Don't follow the 'to let go and go with the flow' mindset, it often aggravates the uncertainty further.
2. Acknowledge the guilt of not being present in the moment, to be present in the moment.
3. Take a moment to slow down the rush by focusing on you breathing with counts. Inhale deeply, feel the sharp intake of air and exhale slowly, counting down four to one.

By bringing focus to these reminders and breathe, you regain control to not react and find balance in the storm of anxiety.

14. Uncertainty is the only certainty

Anxious communication is often masked as a version of positivity. When we struggle to accept our reality, our aversion heightens and we take great lengths to try to avoid the discomforting feeling and/or try to convince ourselves to "be grateful", " be positive", "stay good and all will be positive" and more. We have conditioned ourselves to think by kidding ourselves into positivity, or pretending the discomfort will go away. This is a type of coping mechanism and a false hope.

It feels like a party pooper to our desire to feel good.

When this happens, we often skip the most important steps before attempting positivity. Here is what you can do to not get constantly into a spiral:

1. Lean away from using cliché phrases that offer false security. For example, don't force gratitude if it results in guilt or shame to not connect with positivity.
2. Recognise that the desire for control is a façade – breathe in the desire, exhale, give it space for the feeling to control reduces.
3. Every situation has different people, different expectations, hopes and assumptions, so old ways won't always reap comforting results every time.

By practicing these steps, you can allow yourself to shift perspective, apply honest gratitude and shift the control, to accept that uncertainty is the only certainty.

15. Tame confusion

When faced with unclear situations, an untamed mind clouds itself with judgments and doubts and in this modern world, it makes it much harder for us to see the clarity between the clouds.

Our habit has become to search for information through friends or social media posts, who may not understand an entire situation. Instead of examining our reasons for doubts and judgments, we are concerned about seeking the "good" answer. No one wants to 'screw up'.

Trusting ourselves does not mean coming to the "correct" answer, instead it's about sitting quietly inside and using our negativity as a source of information to return back to our inner wisdom.

To find clarity in the confusion:

1. Resist sitting quietly with confusion. See what has been compromised by our need for others approval or recognition.
2. Pause and listen carefully to the voice that doesn't criticise, judge or convince you.
3. Don't hasten a decision, consider what truly matters in the confusion. Allow the wave of information to pass through you. See what is useful and then drop what isn't.
4. If seeking advice from others, be honest. Before asking, prepare with knowing what is truly in your best interest and that of the other parties involved to talk about your concerns clearly.
5. Notice if you are imparting information that only suits your personal agenda. Ask yourself if you are seeking approval or recognition, because half-truth creates more harm.

Tame the confusion, reduce the overwhelm, find the ease to organise your thoughts.

16. Find clarity in the preferences

In times of complexity, challenges or uncertainty, it's natural to feel internal conflicts. Particularly when different perspectives are present. A perspective is made up of a collection of preferences: values, expectations, hopes and assumptions.

To find the clarity, break the perspective down:

1. Expectations: hidden, spoken, or unspoken - what are the expectations influencing the situation?
2. Assumptions: are there any unspoken assumptions shaping your perspective?
3. Values: which values are being tested and causing internal conflict?
4. Hopes: what outcome are you aiming for and have you communicated this effectively?

17. Commit to checking-in

We are hardest on ourselves then others. This makes it really tough to look at our circumstances clearly.

Consistently practice this:

1. Be aware of the tone and emotional energy in your voice as you approach the situation.
2. Monitor the language in your internal dialogue for signs of self-pressure or disappointment.
3. Notice any physical tightness or tension in your body, indicating resistance, coping mechanisms, or defensiveness.

By intentionally listening to our physical sensations and senses over time, we notice the quality of our discomforting emotions, and by breaking them down, we can interact respectfully with others.

Check-in

18. Recognise aversion

If you really want to have a solid relationship with others, be true about your aversions.

When we are true about them to ourselves, we see how they frame the way we see life.

Aversions are dislikes that are visible in our forms of judgment. Strong dislikes include attachment, pride, arrogance, ignorance, resentment, jealousy, envy and the list goes on. Buried underneath them are deep fears such as: rejection, shame, abandonment or guilt. They feel like inner monsters.

1. Ill will manifests as qualities of anger, hatred and resentment towards ourselves and others, often leading us to victimise ourselves.
2. Ignorance involves avoiding seeing things as they are or being closed-minded to different perspectives.
3. Attachment is the act of clinging to identities, thoughts and situations in order to avoid acknowledging the reality of change and potential opportunities.
4. Pride can manifest in a desire for self-importance and self-worth, leading to harm to ourselves and others.

When we practice calming our physical body, it becomes easier to sit with our aversions, which are like monsters lurking in the shadow. Instead of treating them as a monster, we invite them to share with information we may not have wanted to attend to in the past.

By noticing them, as a kind of informer, don't seek for a lesson, instead find the realisation of why aversions exist in the first place. By doing so, it opens our opportunity to respond to our current situations appropriately and not like we have done in the past.

19. Rise above - uncovers truth

Liberating ourselves from the qualities of aversion starts with seeing it as a source of information.

Untamed aversion is a critical inner voice, constantly judging, through comparison and competition with yourself or with others. Since we don't like how it makes us feel, especially in front of others, we put on a façade so that no one will notice.

If we unpack the critical voice, it's a collection of yesterday's experiences from passed heritage, childhood, even the kind of social engagements in our lives. As our senses constantly absorb this information, together it shapes our thoughts and behaviours without conscious awareness.

So, when we practice confronting this, at first it feels like a brick wall of information, that has been building for years and years of unprocessed information. Processing the information, in smaller doses, we create wider perspective.

Here are some ways to attain this:

1. Journal intentionally. Document your experiences on a regular basis and visit them at a later date. It's measurable and serves as a time-line.
2. Take note about how you distract yourself or avoid quiet moments to escape aversion. Keep check on the number of times you say you are busy, for example.
3. Document the lies you tell yourself, as they can bury a truth you're avoiding. Ask yourself what you fear losing by confronting the truth and what you stand to gain.

By letting yourself look at these moments at a later stage, you can see the small details that you didn't know you missed that made all the difference. And by doing so you can now leverage your aversion by seeing it from a different perspective.

Fyi, keep the journal in a safe and sacred place.

20. Divorce the inner victim

In the event aversion makes you feel like a victim - file for a divorce.

If you find yourself feeling like a victim, it's time to break free from that mindset. A victim mentality is like being in a relationship with a partner who constantly needs to be taken care of, even though you wish you didn't have to deal with them.

When you approach life with a victim mentality, it can feel like there is no hope and it becomes difficult to accept feedback or evaluate situations objectively to take a courageous step in a different direction. Victims tend to blame others or situations for their circumstances and struggle to take responsibility for their own actions.

To overcome this mindset, start paying attention to the words you use when interacting with others. Notice if you frequently use limiting words like "I know", "but", "should", or "can't". Write these words down to make them more tangible and real instead of trying to figure it out mentally alone.

By replacing these limiting words with more empowering ones, such as changing 'but' to 'and', you can shift your perspective and take control of your own narrative.

Remember, you don't have to be a victim in your own life. If the aversion mindset is making you feel stuck, it may be time to 'file for a divorce' from that way of thinking.

21. Take a stand - own your choices

You are always responsible for your moments, and experiences. It's such a hard tablet to swallow and to accept, especially when we are in the process of growing out of victim mode.

Be sure to catch this one thing:

Avoid hiding behind other people's words.

Sometimes we use other people's words, such as their advice or their suggestion, as the reason why a certain action was taken and it didn't work out favourably. But what had really happened was the fear of taking a stand for one's own true decision or action, in case others don't agree, like or approve of it.

Hiding behind other people's words are a way to play it safe, but also a way to avoid taking responsibility for what we truly feel. When it comes to making decisions or making a choice, we struggle or deflect so that we don't get blamed and seen to be a failure.

What can be done:

1. Ask questions. People are more willing to help than we realise.
2. Drop justifying your reasons why you can't do it.
3. Practice failing - it trains the nerves to get comfortable in the discomfort.
4. Taking responsibility for our words and actions is a powerful step.

22. Don't compete, don't compare

It's important to be honest with yourself about your hidden agenda. Sometimes, we may not even realize that we have one, or we may be reluctant to admit that feelings of jealousy or envy are at play.

For example, have you ever felt it, when others have a dream or a desire that looks similar to yours? The only different is they are doing something about it. You may feel sneakily jealous or envious and start comparing your own to theirs, which may reflect as a way to downplay their unique values.

Other times, we will look at another person's achievement and dismiss it by making remarks, or give unsolicited advice. Between these are many shapes that often come across like a competition match.

But the truth is, everyone has their own unique needs and desires, even the most altruistic individuals. The key is tapping into them. So instead of diminishing others joy, to amplify the self-importance or elevate one's own sense of inner pride:

1. Start by acknowledging our own unfulfilled desires with honesty. Realise that we all share the desire to want our desires fulfilled.
2. Don't pretend to be joyful for others if you can't see your own joyfulness.
3. Stop diminishing your own achievements, even the tiniest one's matter. Once we do, we uplift others along the way.
4. Use that feeling of aversion as motivation to take purposeful steps towards achieving the life you secretly desire.
5. Define how you want to feel and shape your mindset to align your actions and emotions towards

a more fulfilling life.
6. By removing the need to compare and competing, we can approach each other with humility and on an equal footing.

23. Open intentionally

Be open with your intentions and any hidden agenda in communications.

Practice being transparent with yourself consistently to reveal the hidden traps that may have been causing unnecessary problems.

Ask yourself:

1. Maybe it's the desire for self-importance, recognition, growing at the expense of others? By being open with yourself, you can cut tendencies that drive your inner guilts and shames.
2. What insecurities are present? By examining it look for why the hidden agenda exists in the first place.
3. Is it pride, envy and jealousy that are influencing your actions and behaviour? Is it coming from a place of malice? How will you act, eventually it affects others on their own path?

By asking deep questions, we come in touch with the unresolved feelings, they no longer serve as a source of protection but as a source of information to change the way we want to connect with others.

24. Path to trust

We all desire a sense of fulfilment and joy in life, to feel we're on the right track.

But when our path diverges from others, self-doubt can creep in, especially when challenges arise. We sense the loneliness of walking our own path, and when we struggle to tame our doubts or the desire to seek validation, our search for reassurance also escalates.

Trying to walk our own path while also feeling part of a community is a balancing act. Reflect on how can we be ourselves while also being part of a community and notice which unique attributes will be frowned upon, if we showed it.

The key is to practice building a healthy relationship and normalise our attitude around the existence with discomfort.

1. By examining the quality of our thoughts regularly, our inner confidence grows, because we are not resisting to change them.
2. We accept them for being there.
3. We no longer feel the need to prove ourselves when surrounded by those who don't always agree with our sets of beliefs and values.

This is the biggest first step: the acceptance.

25. Liberating the inner trust

Commit to discovering your own truth:

1. See the perfectionist tendencies - striving to not make mistakes or fail. Notice the quality of the inner voice when it does fail and how it tries to fix you, compare itself to some perfect imagined version and most of all what is the quality of the inner speech, is it aggressive or passive aggressive? Can the perfectionist tendencies give room to see the self-judgment behind the 'busy' or 'hustle' mindset, and notice what causes the harshness?
2. Relax from constant pretending, take the time to familiarise with your insecurities. Take on a sensitive approach like a parent speaking to a hurt child. By taking on a more patient and listening nature, we can question the root of the insecurity? What is causing the urge to compare? What is the fear of not knowing what the right action step to take is?
3. Recognise if there is a constant feeling of pressure to conform and improve to fit in with a certain culture. Notice if it deprives you of feeling at peace and question if the insecurity is based on needing others people's approval because your set of values conflict with theirs.

By seeing these insecurities over and over without giving it importance, you prioritise your own truth, you give space to see situations with a fresh pair of lenses.

As you continue to realise this, the comparisons to others will no longer hold power over you. Your newfound wisdom can be shared through storytelling, inspiring others to embrace their own truths.

26. Releasing the clinging grip

Being attached to our outcomes, desires and needs, can make life very rigid and often harder to move forward or be open in the relationships that matter.

When we try to mould our outer circumstances and individual preferences to meet our expectations, we risk damaging our relationships over time, which often leads to disagreements, arguments and intense clashes.

To release the grip:

1. By honest to yourself - always come back to owning inner beliefs, expectations, hopes, and biases.
2. Recognise the personal discomfort - that another's differing views challenge your version of truths.
3. See the nature of resistance towards them: does your attitude look defensive, justifying or protective? Question if you are resisting shutting out others due to fear of the unfamiliar while holding onto your beliefs, instead using them to benefit everyone involved.
4. Are you focusing on being right versus considerate. Examine why you may view your truth as superior to others', or cling to your moral standards as inherently better. While you may the urge to resist examining yourself, seeing this allows you to apply a path for possibilities, you would not usually consider.
5. Practice thoughtfulness and discernment to strengthen your ability to receive differing views with an open-mind and clear heart.

27. Respect yourself - respect others

Exploring self-importance and self-worth in conversations

In this world, to be seen as selfish is 'bad'. But so is feeling worthless and diminishing our dignity. What is confused in the narrative around selfish is the balance between self-importance and self-worth. On a spectrum selfish can go between coming across as a people-pleaser or a narcissist and the full range in between. We are looking for something from those individuals: a validation, recognition, acknowledgment, or a similar quality that reflects a form of security about one's self.

When we have low self-importance - it's easy to allow ourselves to be taken advantage of and not know how to set healthy boundaries.

When we have low self-worth, we belittle our own values and unique qualities, where we often don't get recognised for them.

When there is excessive importance or high worth it can easily belittle others' feelings, strip their dignity or respect in favour of personal gain. It makes for conversations around the self and leaves little room to consider others, and the impact of our words and attitude.

When we communicate with others, and these feelings are present, it looks like is a quality of: pride, arrogance and ignorance.

So always, always check in. Inquire into your insecurity of being yourself. By doing this you begin invite a healthy balance in your desire for self-importance, self-worth or self-esteem.

Then assess your nature of self-importance and self-worth in communication with others, by inquiring:

1. Was I assertive without being overbearing?
2. Did I listen actively to others' perspectives?
3. How did I make others feel during our conversation?
4. In what ways can I improve my self-worth and self-importance in future interactions?

This kind of self-inquiry can over time support you to be respectful to yourself and others.

28. Check in with yourself

Did you know that pride, arrogance or ignorance affect our connections with others, more than we wish to reveal?

These three qualities often mask themselves by feelings of resentment, jealousy and envy stemming from unfulfilled part of self. How do you recognise them:

1. Let go of keeping up appearances that hide your truth.
2. Notice when your words or body language and tone of voice seem be trying too hard to make a false impression.
3. Be honest about wanting what others have. Admitting this relieves guilt and shame.
4. Identify the unmet expectations and suppressed desires causing these feelings.
5. Thank the pretension for making you realise what you felt you wanted to experience.

Look inward at how these three qualities prevent you from feeling yourself in any conversation.

29. Pride should uplift, not diminish

Pride is a complex concept revolving around self-respect and appreciation of one's dignity. It is a delicate balance that can empower or harm, depending on the situation.

Defined as a sense of satisfaction derived from one's achievements or qualities, pride is considered positive when based on accomplishments without demeaning others.

Pride can arise from achieving goals through effort and perseverance.

For marginalised communities seeking to reconnect with ancestral cultures hidden due to oppression, pride involves no longer hiding one's truths and embracing what makes one unique.

However, pride can manifest negatively as arrogance, ignorance, or feeling satisfaction at the expense of others. When such pride becomes mistaken pride, step back and pivot, by:

1. Don't use politeness to avoid the moment.
2. Don't let false pride deceive you into acting like a know-it-all and making others feel insignificant.
3. Acknowledge when false pride has harmed another, whether intentionally or unintentionally.
4. Pause to respond with genuine humility, ask questions before imposing your view.
5. Create breathing space to reflect and provide others with the opportunity to do the same.
6. Pivot, take a single minute, to consider pride's positive purpose and consequence for yourself and others. You want to be respectful in the way you stand your ground without being confrontational.

7. When responding, find a balance in your choices of words, to change the way you speak to another person.

People always remember how you make them feel.

30. Break up knowing it all

Arrogance and ignorance are subtle obstacles that prevent us from connecting genuinely with others, even when we believe we want to understand their differences and views.

When we are arrogant, we enter conversations thinking we already know it all rather than staying curious and opening-minded. Think about the feeling of entitlement when we complain about not getting what we deserve.

Ignorance, on the other hand, lacks the desire for awareness of our limitations in grasping different perspectives. It has the 'as long as it doesn't affect me, why should I care' vibe.

Both come from a closed mentality and sense of superiority over others' struggles -like managing to insult someone without realising it. If you want to see this quickly: observe how we speak to someone serving us at a restaurant.

When our self-importance plays a greater role in the conversation, it hinders others' feeling of safety to express themselves and shut down.

The key is a humble beginner's mind approach in any interaction by checking in for:

1. Complacency - when things seem fine on the surface and there is a lack of incentive to self-reflect or consider other viewpoints, trapping us in our comfort zones. As long it doesn't affect one's life there is no need to change, even if it's at the cost of another's life.
2. Superiority - feeling above others' problems stems from lacking understanding that everyone faces challenges. Interfering in other people's beliefs and

ways of being without assessing level of appropriateness.
3. Avoidance - sidestepping complicated conversations leading to the reluctance to acknowledge difficult relational truths. Avoiding recognising personal responsibility even if the action had caused another harm.

Appling this in our modern world of rapid changes, what was true yesterday is not necessarily true for tomorrow. When we drop the knowing it all, it stretches us to see into our assumptions and biases gracefully, while supporting us to broaden our horizons, and build strategic relationships.

Most of all, it allows us to evolve from outdated thinking and create space for innovative solutions, with greater ease.

31. Cancel regret of regrets

To understand regrets, we have to understand the relationship with regrets. Regrets are the failure to have acted upon something in the past and wishing we had done it so that our present day would feel different. But is it necessary to have regrets?

How would we be if regrets did not exist? Regrets are waking up moments, for us to reflect back into the nature of our manners, our comfort zone, and our pride.

Because life is so transitional, we fail to realise by avoiding some conversations or not having taken that one action, when life brings unexpected change such as a death of a loved one, the 'no' to a business venture or not taking the leap to go on that life time trip, we look back and feel "I wish I had done that".

But by regretting, we also fail to see the beauty of where we are at this moment. Regrets are a reflection of our desire to control and by relinquishing our feelings of regret we move closer towards accepting our moments as they are.

So, the next time you find yourself feeling regret, cancel the regret because yesterday will not arrive and tomorrow will remain uncertain.

32. Life is a constant transition

No one is born perfect or instantly great, we all grow from our imperfections and from uncertainty. This is reality.

Uncertainty will always challenge our comfort zone, and it's ever present. So, in many ways, we live in a constant state of transition, where every moment is a beginning and an end, every moment is perfect and imperfect. And as our outer circumstances keep evolving, we will as well. So, why strive for perfection?

How do we define perfectionism and what guarantee is the method of control going to reap the outcome you wish?

No one person has ever lived the life they exactly predicted it to be. In fact, by trying to achieve this, it blindfolds us from appreciating and embracing life's constant evolution and growth. Just like the seasons of weather.

By liking comfort and disliking discomfort, we make our personal path to living harmoniously with ourselves difficult. We spend time thinking about controlling our tomorrow, and regretting our yesterday, and in between trying to solve, fix or complain. We fail to maximise our present moment.

But if we allow ourselves to see life as a transition, instead of tripping over our expectations and disappointments we leverage them to make the most out of our moments and experience life fully:

Here are a few ways you can leverage your transitions:

1. Understand your capabilities.
2. Evaluate your relationship with risk.

3. Recognise limitations and assumptions.
4. Reflect on and adapt to the unexpected.
5. Discover hidden passions.
6. Transform how to communicate, engage and consider others in your environment.
7. Revise often- transitions are ever-evolving

By embracing the role they play in our growth, we release perfectionistic pressures, feeling more open to unexpected opportunities.

33. Open mind – open heart

As we move through our life transitions, staying open-minded and open-hearted, can make all the difference.

By having an open mind and open heart, it's like a tube, wide enough that we no longer cling or fight our different kinds of afflictions, aversions, and attachments. Instead, it's open enough to flow smoothly through life.

By befriending our minds daily, the struggle feels less because we are in our natural awareness. Instead of seeking self-awareness, it's a state of being.

How do we recognise when we are in a state of a mind-open heart?

An open mind involves willingly engaging with fresh ideas, putting aside judgment or preconceived ideas. This signifies releasing our fixation on pre-established beliefs, thus allowing us to embrace different viewpoints and ways of thinking. This openness allows for continuous consideration, deeper understanding and the ability to adapt in the face of change.

An open heart involves cultivating compassion, kindness and empathy towards oneself and others. It means shedding selfishness, resentment, and judgment; approaching ourselves and others with acceptance and understanding.

By resting in the state of acceptance and understanding we are able to look at adversity, choose our attitude and weigh situations without feeling the fear of losing one's calm confidence to express one's authenticity.

34. Your mental dialogue designs your world

A profound truth often overlooked: our persistent mental preoccupations shape our personal reality.

As we become more into our awareness, we become aware how the choices of our reactions and interactions play a part in the environment.

For example, some individuals who are afraid of financial scarcity, may have a tendency to hoard and speak their fears about the world persistently.

But by becoming aware of our discomforts, we notice how we phrase sentences, the quality of words chosen, the tone conveyed and on how this shapes our reality over time.

Going back to the example, an individual who keeps talking about scarcity, has to first recognise they're speaking from scarcity, they make decisions from that mindset.

So, it's our interpretation that is designing our world.

To stay aware, we want to pay attention to deliberately choose how we speak about ourselves and to others:

Do this by:

1. Utilising your thoughts as an information gatherer.
2. Regulating your emotions consciously.
3. Tracking how certain words make you feel and how you apply them in conversation.
4. Minimising diminishing vocabulary and the urge to defend yourself rashly.
5. Pausing to select your language intentionally.

35. Stick with self-examination

Be consistent in examination:

1. Look inward to free yourself from the stress and demands you put on yourself. Prevents burning out.
2. Understand your personal biases and attachments, so that you can build a healthier relationship with yourself.
3. Expand and explore your choice of certain words and define them. Notice if it makes room to see things differently when you face new situations.
4. Accept your unique voice with confidence, it's free from feeling self-conscious.
5. You can choose how you want to be in a relationship as long as it's with a healthy pride and care for yourself and others.
6. Release the need to please others and pretend to be someone else, set clear boundaries.
7. Look at your actions with appreciation and authenticity.

36. Be selective in your consumption

Be careful with how much you learn. If you know too much or too little, it can change how your dynamics of communication with others.

When you know too much, people may not understand you if your language has too much jargon or complexity.

Reading books, especially in the self-development or academic genre, may seem excellent, but if you don't use what you learn, it can be a burden. You may struggle to share the knowledge purposefully, because it lacks one's experience.

While having knowledge has been praised as a way to look smart, it doesn't necessarily mean it's understood.

Act on your knowledge wisely:

1. Treat knowledge like a tool: use it, flex it and explore it.
2. Read the room. Notice who you are sharing the knowledge with, how much do they know about this knowledge.
3. Then edit it, select what is important, useful and valuable.
4. Let others get involved, recognise the different realisations gained from the experience.
5. Finally, get bored with your knowledge. When the knowledge become lived practice, there won't be a need to aggrandize it.

Once you do that, the knowledge no longer serves you. It can serve others. You will have the wisdom of how to share it in different spaces.

37. You are the power of choice

You don't have a choice - you are a choice. There will always be events and circumstances outside of your control. What matters most is how you choose to respond.

If you react in ways that diminishes self-respect, this can hold you back later in life when challenges arise.

However, if you can detach from unhelpful thoughts and maintain resilience, you will be better equipped to make the most of every moment, no matter what comes your way.

Big or small, the challenges you face can be better handled if you build the habits now. Apply self-compassion and flexibility of thought. Recognise in this moment that you are a choice in how you react, or respond.

Choose the one that you fear the most but gives least resistance.

38. The four P's guide

When it's time to see your choices and make decisions.

These four P's can guide you:

1. The most important P is your principles. Your principles are like a built-in GPS, guiding your behaviours and choices. They're a reflection of your values, and act as a personal compass. Understanding and living by your principles can promote personal growth and meaningful relationships with others, despite differing viewpoints.

Ask yourself: what are the fundamental truths I live by? What fuels my actions?
Having clarity about your principles ensures that your decisions sync with your value system.

The next 3 P's are like the pillars of sound decision-making:
Priorities, position and preferences

2. Priorities are your most pressing responsibilities; be clear which one matters the most.

Ask yourself: what are your immediate responsibilities or commitments?
Identifying priorities helps you pay attention to what's crucial at the moment.

3. Your position is the influence you hold in a situation. Recognising this allows thoughtful assessment of how actions may affect others.

Ask yourself: how much sway do you have over this

situation?
In what way does my position and my actions impact others?

4. Preferences reveal your true wants and wishes in any circumstance. Identifying these provides insight into motivations.

Ask yourself: what do you lean towards or desire? What preferences do you really need to be true about.

With these 'Four Ps', we're better equipped to make thoughtful choices. It builds understanding of perspectives, concerns and motivations while searching for agreeable solutions.

39. Refresh and repeat

It's easy to fall back into old habits when we feel we've made progress or get comfortable and complacent.

But life is funny, it's unpredictability can happen anytime, especially in relationships. When we are too complacent, some relationships may fall apart, arguments may arise and more.

Such situations can lead us to question ourselves anew - and that's entirely acceptable. Quit being harsh with 'I know that' instead,

Return to the beginning:

1. Remember the agreement you made with yourself to stop kidding yourself when adversity appears.
2. Re-examine the emotions you feel towards the relationship. Reflect on the qualities of thoughts, sentiments, and tendencies that may have re-emerged.
3. Allow yourself to release any feelings of guilt for not being on the same page as the other party in the relationship.
4. Resist the urge to prematurely terminate the relationship. Instead, focus on discerning the actual cause of your discomfort from your thoughts to see the situation objectively.
5. Acknowledge what no longer holds valid in your relationship. It's not uncommon for certain relationships to outlive their usefulness due to evolving dynamics between individuals and having irreconcilable differences.
6. Refreshing the process can serve as a guide in identifying the root cause of your unease and formulate a clear way to communicate it.

40. Quiet intentionally

The power to be quiet inside is, in fact, your greatest asset when navigating various communication scenarios; however, it must never be used as a weapon of silent hostility or as a manipulative tactic. This has damaging repercussions.

Establish a foundation of quiet strength to guide you to:

1. Connect more profoundly within yourself, get back to your principles and priorities.
2. Listen to others without the interruption of your judgments.
3. Streamline your empathetic language with others. Relax from the urge to control the narrative of another.
4. Retain a composed demeanour, even when confronted with undesirable sentiments.

41. What you don't know that you don't know

Our minds will always relax into assumptions when relating to familiar people.

We presume to know how someone thinks or feels and easily fall into the comfort of judgments. Yet more happens within a person than we realise. So, when relational disruptions happen, it's easy to fall into quick reactions.

To avoid this:

1. Treat awkward moments by pausing to rediscover those you think you know.
2. Recognise that time and life alter for every individual between each encounter.
3. It's easy to become pre-occupied with ourselves and assume others already perceive our changes.
4. Slow down and lessen the need to justify your assumptions and expectations. It often escalates into an argument.
5. Steer the mind from being in a place of assuming towards a place of not knowing, being understanding and having patience.
6. Suspend your opinion in favour of thoughtful questions and actively listen to uncover what remains unsaid.

Make it a standing invitation to yourself to approach matters of the heart with deliberate mindfulness.

42. Have a relational authenticity

Having real relationships with all kinds of people has many benefits.

One of the greatest benefits is that we begin to see how our authenticity can fluctuate in energy and pace, depending on who we are surrounded with in the moment.

By spending time on relationships with people who don't necessarily see life the way we do:

1. It invites us to have a more open-minded, caring, and thoughtful approach
2. It helps us shift perspective by understanding new views.
3. It inspires us to appreciate similarities and differences in others
4. It helps us listen to real opinions from others, not just compliments.
5. It gives us a chance to explore who we are and how we talk and recognise inner qualities we hadn't considered.
6. We are more fluid in connecting with others, by adapting and sharing our stories.
7. We are at ease to make a conscious choice to adjust our behaviour appropriately.
8. We stop being scared of surrounding ourselves with people who think differently, and become more considerate.

43. Seek wisdom in those you meet

Remarkably, it's often the people you least expect who may offer the wisdom, encouragement or expertise you need most.

Cultivating a diverse set of connections is invaluable, so be thoughtful in choosing your relationships for learning.

Choose people who carry the wisdom and are aligned with their integrity, not because of their status. In essence, it's the relationships we engage with often that sculpt us, influencing our worldview.

Choose wisely - be thoughtful and intentional. Those who surround you should challenge you, provide motivation and lift your spirits. Look for qualities that:

1. Encourage self-reflection, inspire humility and empower you to understand and confront your flaws.
2. Provide a fresh perspective on your beliefs and values, enabling you to see your failings, flaws, and weaknesses as opportunities for growth and progress.
3. Offer you opportunities to learn and master skills they have already honed.

44. Find consideration in the complexity

When faced with difficulty and conflict due to different opinions, situations can seem overwhelming.

We may not know how to balance our own needs, other people's needs and our different moral values. Neither side really wants to hurt anyone with words or by actions. But yet we may find ourselves thinking what is 'right', what is 'wrong' or 'bad'.

Move from thinking duality and reflect on consideration. Consider what is the consequences of our perspectives. What is harm, harmful, or beneficial for our ourselves and others.

The idea of causing harm comes when we consider our own perspectives are more important than others'. Harm can happen when we manipulate or overlook others. This is not unfamiliar in different heritages.

The key is to see that every discomforting situation is a source of value and to understand this. Find common ground.

It starts by conditioning our minds to:

1. Understand each person's intentions, needs and goals.
2. Attend to our own needs and goals, while also being true about our need for self-importance.
3. Establish on what can already be agreed on as common ground to navigate the differences.

45. Examine intention

The road to understanding good intentions.

We all have good intentions, but sometimes our desire to interfere can backfire. Often when we interfere in others' choices or decisions, our 'help' may not be appreciated as we expected. it's easy to get offended and defensive.

Good intentions are complex.

Sometimes it's not that we are really wanting to help another as much as it's about comforting someone to fit our version of comfort. The reality is that good intentions can cloud sound judgment. What we may see as morally good, another may not necessarily view the same way. This often happens in different ethnic communities, religions, political climates and more.

When we feel pressure to conform to a specific moral view, it can lead to self-doubt, inner turmoil and reluctance to speak freely. When we pressure others with our strong moral beliefs, it comes across as forcing our way on others, causing tension. At its extreme we have polarised views.

When we have difficulties seeing situations clearly and considering other perspectives, we want to check in with our idea of 'doing good'.

1. What does good mean?
2. Do I understand where others are coming from?
3. Who really does this benefit?
4. What questions do I need to ask to shape my actions to be beneficial?

It's best to have true intentions, be open to examining your own self-interest, before stepping in to guide another's situation. And when deciding to have discussions around morality keep consideration, respect and dignity at the forefront.

46. Prepare for the unprepared

To understand any complex conversation, it requires preparation.

Have a simple rule: keep it simple - observe more than you speak - understand before acting.

1. Cultivate patience to not always fill the silence as a way to drive one's self-interest.
2. Strive for self-awareness of how you pick up on the unspoken wants, needs, and ideas in yourself and others.
3. Understand their communication style - the tone, the body language, the moments of thoughtfulness, protectiveness or concern.
4. Notice how you and others respond to the purpose and needs of the conversation.
5. By paying close attention, weigh your answers and disagreements to find the appropriate choice of communication.

47. Lead as an open example

Being at ease with your own flaws and imperfections can make the atmosphere comfortable for others. When we enter a space defensively or rigidly adhere to a predetermined plan, it can challenge the room's sense of safety.

Lead by example in your attitude and demeanour:

1. Practice calm and humility within yourself to not be in a rush to react.
2. Practice awareness that different perspectives may cause others to feel afraid or apprehensive to speak openly if they aren't accustomed to it.
3. Observe the differences to see what looks like barriers and boundaries. This helps establish common ground and what is non-negotiable.
4. Don't force inclusivity on people with different views. What's inclusive for you may not necessarily be for others, instead propose the inclusivity.
5. Avoiding differences or being inauthentic only makes things worse.
6. Stay purposeful, seek reason to engage with dialogue.
7. Pace your articulation respectfully.

48. Get over yourself

When another person is communicating, it is important to keep in mind three key reminders:

1. Be patient: it is crucial to be patient and fully attentive while listening to others. Avoid interrupting or jumping to conclusions, allowing the speaker to express themselves without feeling rushed or dismissed.
2. Don't take it personal: understand that the words spoken by others may not always be directed at you personally. Consider different perspectives and avoid reacting defensively, as it may hinder open and honest communication.
3. Don't take it for granted: respect the value of what others are sharing with you. Acknowledge their thoughts and feelings and show appreciation for their perspective by actively listening and responding thoughtfully.
4. Don't freeze: don't remain stuck when one of your thoughts and opinions feel attacked. Breathe to continue to listen without focusing on replying.

By practicing this style of listening, you gain insight to what's meaningful and impactful for those around you.

49. Consider yourself when considering others

There is often a profound confusion in the minds of people between being thoughtful of other's feelings and bending backward to please everyone around them. This confusion springs from the fear of not seeming 'considerate enough'. When this happens:

1. It's possible to lose touch with your true self and struggle to assert your own beliefs, values and opinions for fear of disagreement.
2. It involves a hidden desire to seek validation from others without considering the costs of constantly bending to their will.
3. Eventually both suppressed authenticity and not being fully validated surface as forms of resentment, jealousy and other negative emotions.

Practice this instead:

1. Understand your own preferences, concerns and boundaries. Check in with your expectations, they can be tricky and conflicting, especially, if they seek the comfort of recognition.
2. Then consider others' preferences and find areas of agreement to understand how to respect the differences.
3. Strive for consideration - take the time to weigh in each other's differences, purpose and desired outcome, by considering what is important, meaningful, and valuable.

By considering and respecting the differences between yourself and others, you can avoid the guilt of not always agreeing and maintain a more assertive and self-assured stance in your interactions.

50. Stand firm gracefully

When it comes to boundaries in complex conversations, defining them can feel like a challenge and look like a barrier.

Before going further, practice the truth to know what is the difference between a boundary and a barrier.

A boundary is preventative, it's consistent and aligned with your principles and values. A barrier has a protective quality, it fluctuates between relationship to relationship.

It's important to discern between the two, it will help you stay calm when conversing in complex matters.

Here are some ways to tackle this:

1. Your boundaries are just as valuable as others'. Even if the power of decision-making lies with the other person, understand what you are boundaries are so that you do not compromise them.
2. Be wise in a conversation and don't allow yourself to be dominated by another perspective out of fear of having a differing view. If someone tries to overwhelm you with their opinions and points of view being the right ones, be okay with disagreeing. Disagreement doesn't have to be impolite or met with a tone of aggression.
3. Establish if the person is willing to listen. If they are not, excuse yourself and come back to the conversation later, if it's necessary and has value.
4. Stay true to yourself and don't compromise expressing your values for the sake of keeping the peace.
5. Have key phrases ready that do not diminish your self-respect, such as "thank you for sharing your

perspective" or "I appreciate your time. I will...".
Reframe your responses to show gratitude without
fear of disrespect.

6. Find a balance between being too friendly and
   unfriendly. You don't have to please others through
   fake agreement just to be polite.

Remember that setting boundaries and standing up for
yourself in difficult conversations is important. Stand
your ground respectfully and confidently.

51. Stay purposeful in your intention

Stay focused on the purpose of the conversation. It's easy to become distracted when our emotions are triggered by the topic at hand. We may find ourselves getting caught up in minor details, fuelled by our own sense of pride. Think about moments in a disagreement when the past was brought up as an example, and doesn't hold much relevancy in the current dialogue.

When engaging in dialogue, it's important to:

1. Approach the situation with gentleness and a clear understanding of the intended goal.
2. Utilize transitional phrases such as "I understand," "I noticed," or "I can see where that may..." to show empathy as a way to acknowledge the other person's perspective and follow with up with a 'permission' style question: "may I offer a suggestion..."
3. Be mindful of using words like 'but' or 'must', as they can come across as dismissive of the other person's feelings. By being mindful of our words and actions, we can ensure that the dialogue remains constructive and respectful.

Remember to stay present and steer the conversation back towards its true purpose.

52. Words matter

Pay attention to the choice of your words - they matter.

Words hold power and influence, shaping not only ourselves but also those around us. Each word and each sentence carries weight, freeing us from the burden of pretending to be someone we're not. To choose wisely in any different circumstance:

1. Make sure you don't overlook the significance of our beliefs, values and the impact of our messages. If we don't do this, the way we speak may jeopardise the safety feeling in a conversation.
2. Notice the kind of words we express surrounding our personal beliefs:

If we are too rigid and closed off to alternative viewpoints, our vocabulary may be peppered with dismissive or careless words that diminish others and make them feel small. Our tone may be short and sharp. Phrases often include: "must", "should", and "have to".

On the flip side, if we are afraid to share our beliefs, we often find ourselves adding unnecessary filler words before expressing our true thoughts, feeling self-conscious about how our messages will be received. Cushioning our views with "I think", "I don't how you feel".

3. Be a great listener. Observe the quality and type of the words, metaphors, analogies and cultural expressions present in complex conversations. By doing so, we can gracefully leverage them to support one another without the fear of making a mistake.

Prioritise being patient with your authenticity and remember words are a creative tool. Spend time exploring words, describing situations differently to different people. This will stretch your calmness to choose how to express your authenticity, with integrity and sincerity, when you least expect it.

53. Feedback is a gift, handle it with care

If you find yourself being hard on yourself, try not to be harsh with others. It's important to take a step back and understand what may be influencing your self-judgment, so that you don't project it on others.

If we are careless with the responsibility that comes with feedback and criticism, it's impact can stick in someone's mind, be carried by them for life.

Instead, reflect on how you would like feedback to be delivered to you - how do you want it to impact your confidence? Negative experiences can be opportunities for growth, so frame your words as invitations or suggestions rather than absolute truths.

1. Prepare to have patience when listening and communicating feedback. Recognise that you are entering their safety zone.
2. Take the time to consider the other person's perspective and approach the situation with sincerity.
3. Avoid sandwiching the feedback in pretty phrases.
4. Start by acknowledging the challenges at hand and asking if they would like to share anything that has been considered.
5. Offer insights and suggestions, beginning with a paraphrase to shows active listening.
6. Provide action steps and plan, focusing on the situation rather than personal criticism.

Always be purposeful in your feedback, recognising the responsibility that comes with offering it. Be purposeful - not personal.

54. Empathy knows no comparison

If there is one word, we use a lot in the world is 'empathy'. While this is a powerful word, it's now used far to often as a way to protect ourselves from feeling the painful moments and when we may not have an answer or way to support someone in life, confusing it as sympathy.

Let's get clear about the difference between the two:

Sympathy shows up when we feel sorry or sad for someone going through a difficult moment which we are currently not experiencing ourselves.

Empathy is when we recognising someone is struggling and suffering from a difficult circumstance and we are placing ourselves in their position to understand their emotions, thoughts and actions.

However, empathy gets blurred:

1. When we start comparing our situations with theirs.
2. Feel the intense desire to have 'good intentions' to get to their solutions.
3. Give unsolicited advice, when situations and perspectives are different.
4. By getting emotionally involved and taking action to support them, without seeing the bigger perspective
5. We become emotionally invested, because we feel it's unfair what another is experiencing and feel a sense of duty to be the solutioner.

As shared in previous slogans, emotions are energy carriers, when we are too caught up in the heavy emotions of others, we may experience fatigue or exhaustion by getting too involved or try to change a situation to suit our way of seeing it.

To truly empathise:

1. Create a safe space for mixed emotions to be discussed.
2. Focus on listening without comparison or adding personal view.
3. Replace advice with paraphrasing- share what you hear and notice.
4. Ask clarifying questions. By doing so, we allow the person experiencing mixed emotions to come to their own understanding and find confidence in their situation.
5. Only get involved when permission is received.

Recognise that empathy is about objective understanding which can be useful for strategic, and meaningful decision-making and planning.

55. Empower others with light-heartedness

Let a sense of humour serve for the better.

1. It's okay to laugh at yourself or share stories about yourself with light humour that will not diminish your self-respect and self-worth.
2. Laugh at your own shortcomings and judgements only if it creates a positive and confident mindset.
3. Share them to motivate others when they are being hard on themselves.
4. But don't give others permission to use your light-heartedness against you.
5. Humour should never come at the expense of someone else.
6. Avoid making inappropriate jokes, even in casual settings.

Be at ease with yourself, and not take yourself all the time too seriously, can make you a shining example of self-assurance to uplift each other.

56. Be genuine

No matter what the disagreements or differences, meet the moment with understanding and respect.

1. Cultivate a genuine interest. Listen attentively to what others value and how they articulate themselves. Notice what level of respect do they have for themselves or their community.
2. Take note of their priorities, such as cultural background, loyalty, family, social standing, friendship, or professional aspirations.
3. Understanding what drives them or motivates them, can inform the way you interact with them.

By making an effort to truly listen and understand others, you make others feel acknowledged and valued, which ultimately reduces barriers to vulnerability and generates a sense of consideration.

57. Not too tight not too loose

Refine your ability to adapt your communication approach across diverse situations, communities and environments without compromising your authentic self.

1. Practice visualisation for different scenarios. Imagine speaking to the different kinds of individuals who influence you in distinct ways. How would you share the same message to your parent, colleague or someone who challenges you.
2. Tune into your emotional undertones in different relationships - observe your vocal tone, word emphasis, pacing and silences - this helps you shape the atmosphere around you, when presented in different circumstances.
3. Practice reading the energy in a room to expand your interaction style. Strive to come from a place of understanding, especially when presenting to different kinds of audiences.
4. Don't be in a hurry to interact, pause-breathe-assess. It takes a short moment, to gather yourself and adjust the tone, pace, and word choices accordingly.

To find the sweet spot in any interaction, remember to be neither too loose nor too tight with your communication style.

58. Stories open doors, not close minds

Storytelling is a valuable tool known to share emotions, empathy and find common ground. Here are some tips on how to use it in talking to diversified communities:

1. Share stories to connect, not prove. Instead of constantly trying to prove your expertise, focus on sharing personal experiences and listening to others' stories.
2. Share stories as if they are realisations moments that made a positive impact in your life.
3. Be selective in the personal stories you choose to share - is it appropriate and respectful?
4. Don't just tell the same stories the same way; seek different ways to share them. One story can have many purposes and meaning. Be open to the wisdom they offer those around you so that you can frame a story to convey the relevant realisations, insights and understandings.
5. Keep the story simple, especially when the community speaks different languages and, when possible, make it interactive so people can feel it.
6. Remember to stay grounded in your beliefs while connecting with others on different levels even through storytelling.

59. Practice, not perfection

Being with each other's differences is challenging. There will always be moments, where we won't reach agreement and have to be 'tolerant' of one another. Stay calm and balanced in those moments takes consistent practice of checking in with ourselves.

Practice equanimity is a powerful skill.

Remember, there is never a perfect way to talk in a clear and peaceful way. So, stay steady when our differences show up.

When we remain composed and steady during conversations, we can better understand others and express ourselves effectively.

The importance is to consistently remind ourselves that we each hold responsibility for our communication, as it is within our control. Regardless of the circumstances we face, we have the power to choose how we behave, respond and engage with the world.

This is how we shape our influence, enact change and leave a lasting impact on the world.

1. Make friends with your communication. It's not a race, but a journey.
2. Enjoy the process; embrace the times when things don't go your way.
3. Extend empathy and remember that people may not meet you exactly where you stand.
4. Champion genuine understanding and approach each situation with a mindset inspired with equanimity.

It's just practice.

Resources

Book 1 #befriendurmind

Available on Amazon-Kindle -Apple.

Follow

Instagram @Kirtana168 & @befriendurmind

Youtube @kirtana168

Podcast Befriend your Mind

Available on Spotify, Apple and more.

For latest updates https://www.kirtana168.com

Printed in Great Britain
by Amazon